IN PRAIS
STRESS FREE T.

CW00968443

Clear, easy to apply, no-nonsense approac   ı
their business more effectively and more profitably. I wish I had this when ı first
started out.

David Hyner, www.davidhyner.com

If you are running your own business, you will have to decide if you wish to
submit a tax return or pay an accountant to do it for you. In this easy to read guide,
Anna Goodwin shows us how Bert and Alan make this decision, and what is required
of them, in particular, how to track and file the information which is essential for an
accurate, compliant tax return. Once you have read this guide, if you had any doubts
about the merits of using an accountant to prepare and submit a return on your
behalf, Anna will have dispelled them, so that you can get on and do what you do
best - run your own business!

Ralph Savage of DRS Business Solutions

The simple drawings and bite size chunks of text enabled me to focus on the stuff
that mattered, rather than trying to understand jargon. A serious bit of information
given in a light hearted and empathic manner. Spot on!

Diane Cleary

I really like how Anna has made this to be simple, fun and manageable. Very easy
to understand which makes life easier - happy days! Thanks Anna for taking the time
to show how tax doesn't have to be so complicated. Great stuff!

Sheila Mc Mahon, Entertainer,
Counsellor and CEO of Mind Management for You

Anna Goodwin is really approachable and helpful and has a real knack of making all things related to accountancy easy to understand and take care of. Her booklets, like Anna herself, walk you through things one step at a time and leave you feeling confident that everything is going to be sorted properly.

Tony Burgess Academy of High Achievers Limited

I love it! Lovely clear explanations, and the graphics are super.

Rebecca Benneyworth, Tax advisor and lecturer

Alan, Bert and the Fairy Godmother make light work of understanding the tax return with their simple and easy to follow step by step guide. A must read for anyone running a business or wanting to understand the process to increase efficiency.

Laura Riley, Level 4 AAT technician student

All clear and straightforward. Makes sense and easy to read.

Matthew Farnsworth of Feltons, Chartered Accountants

STRESS FREE
TAX RETURNS

ANNA GOODWIN

Stress Free Tax Returns
Be better prepared for HMRC and know what to give your accountant and when.

STRESS FREE TAX RETURNS

BE BETTER PREPARED FOR HMRC
AND KNOW WHAT TO GIVE YOUR
ACCOUNTANT AND WHEN.

ANNA GOODWIN

Is this you? Are you stuck now?

This is something that needs to get sorted but where do you start?

Follow me and I'll show you in simple steps!

First things first

1. Gather a big pile of <u>everything</u> that needs sorting together.

2. <u>Absolutely</u> everything – even those bits and bobs you keep avoiding because you don't really know what to do with them.

tip!

Even though you don't want to do this, don't like it, you may as well get on with it as you'll feel better later!

The tax year runs from 6 April each year to the 5 April of the next and will be the period that you are focused on for your income and expenditure.

Is that everything, Bert? Gee, it sure does look a lot!

I wish I'd spent the time filing mine, Alan.

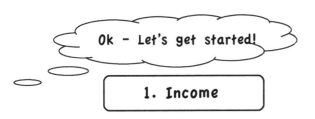

Ok – Let's get started!

1. Income

First thing to get your head around is this is <u>all</u> your income. Imagine a big pot:

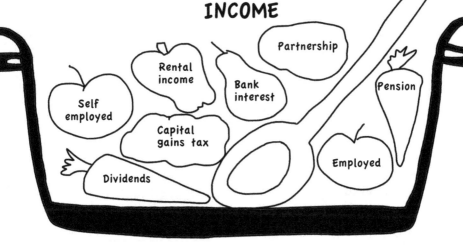

INCOME

Self employed • Rental income • Bank interest • Partnership • Pension • Capital gains tax • Dividends • Employed

You should have evidence for <u>all</u> your income.
This hasn't got to be a full invoice.

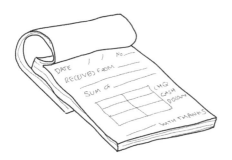

It can be a receipt from a duplicated receipt book.

But you need proof for the whole year!

2. Employed

You will receive a P60 and P11D from your employee by 31st May each year.

Gather together all of the P60's and P11D's from each of your employers.

tip! Check that the P60's are for the correct tax year!

I don't think I need this one Bert!

3. Bank Interest

The easiest is to contact your bank and ask for an interest statement for each of your bank accounts.

Hey Alan, all my interest statements are online!

tip! Yet again, check that you're requesting the correct tax year.

4. Dividend Income

If you have shares you are likely to receive dividends from them. You will need to gather together all of the dividend vouchers for all of your shares.

FILE TIP

File UK and foreign dividend vouchers separately in date order.

tip!
1. You may receive income annually, quarterly, monthly.

2. Income may be from a UK or a foreign company.

5. Pension

This can be pension income from a previous job or a state pension. You may have a few pensions.

Yet again, gather together all the P60's for your pension income.

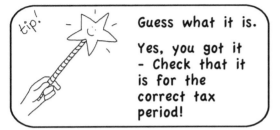

tip!

Guess what it is.

Yes, you got it - Check that it is for the correct tax period!

P60
2012/13

Alan Roller

£0.00

6. Rental Income

You may have one property or you may have several. All rental income from all properties needs to be identified and recorded separately.

You may be managing the properties yourself.

Gather together all your income receipts.

tip!

You should have your income receipts. Even if your tenant doesn't want a copy, keep your copy - it only needs to be from a duplicated receipt book.

You may have an agent.

Gather together all the rental statements for all the properties.

FILE TIP

File the statements for each property separately in date order.

RENTAL STATEMENT June

RENTAL STATEMENT July

RENTAL STATEMENT Aug

RENTAL STATEMENT June

RENTAL STATEMENT July

RENTAL STATEMENT Aug

Property 1
In date order

Property 2
In date order

7. Capital Gains Income

Don't forget, you need to keep details of proceeds made on disposal of, for example, a property which is not your main residence or shares.

tip! Where can you find the annual exemption limit? http:// www.hmrc.gov.uk/ rates/cgt.htm

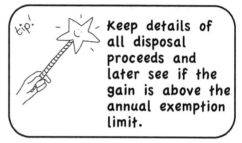

tip! Keep details of all disposal proceeds and later see if the gain is above the annual exemption limit.

Expenditure Now

1. Self Employed / Partnership

You will need all your expenses documentation for the year - this will vary from tiny parking receipts to A4 pieces of paper.

FILE TIP

The easiest way to keep them is to staple all receipts onto an A4 piece of paper and number each one consecutively, starting at 1.

Once you have gathered everything, see the recording section for what to do with them.

tip! Motor expenses: Claim business mileage at 45p per mile (keep a record of all business journeys made) or as a business proportion of all motor expenses.

tip! Entertaining is <u>not</u> allowed. Subsistence re. business meetings is allowed.

2. Employed - Expenses

Some expenses incurred because of work are allowable, for example subscriptions. Details of these are needed.

3. Pension Payments

Pension contributions made to each pension provider are needed.

4. Rental Expenditure

For each property, keep details of expenditure incurred, for example:

- Gas Certificate
- Insurance
- Mortgage Interest
- Legal fees
- Agent fees

Total them for the year – separately for each property.

5. Capital Gains Expenditure

Keep all <u>relevant</u> expenditure for <u>each</u> purchase <u>separately</u>, for example:

- Purchase cost
- Legal fees
- Capital improvements

6. Gift Aid Payments

Payments made to a charity. You have a choice when you make the payment of having your tax claimed on behalf of the charity – gift aid.

List all the payments made for the year separately for each charity and broken down into recurring or one-off ones.

So, why would you use an accountant to complete your tax return?

- Saves you time
- Peace of mind
- Everything done properly; no under or over claims made
- All the HMRC paperwork goes to the agent, as well as you

Payment of Tax Owed

Phew! All done!

When I completed my tax return the tax calculation told me how much to pay, but how do I pay it?

Oh my accountant gave me a list of ways to pay. Do you want me to send it you?

Yes please. Maybe an accountant is useful after all!

Tips for Filing / Recording

INCOME - Filing

IMPORTANT
Choose the system
that suits you.

- Keep all income receipts
- File numerically — start at 1
- File in date order — start at 1st April if your year end is 31st March

INCOME - Recording

- Manually — In a bookkeeping book — list each receipt throughout the month and total at the end of the month.

- Computerised spreadsheet — As above but on the computer.

- Accounting software package — As above but on the computer.

EXPENSES - Filing

- Keep all receipts — If you're not sure they are tax deductible, then ask.

- File numerically — Number them yourself, starting at 1, rather than using the invoice number automatically entered — this is usually massive and you'll waste time writing it out.

- File in date order — Start at 1st April if your year end is 31st March.

EXPENSES - Recording

- Manually
OR - Computerised spreadsheet
OR - Accounting software package

Make a list of each entry, analysed into the relevant expenditure:

- Purchases
- Motor expenses
- Travel including accommodation
- Wages
- Rent, rates, insurance

- Repairs
- Accountancy
- Bank interest / charges
- Telephone
- Stationery

etc. — and total at the end of the month

Good luck with gathering all your information together for your accountant or for your self assessment. In my experience, this helps both you and the accountant as it means you have less queries from your accountant.

Also you will keep more up to date as you know what is needed.

The tax return is due to be submitted by 31st January each year but if you send your information early to your accountant you will have more warning of how much tax you need to pay or you will receive your refund earlier.

Go for it and at least aim to get your information sorted and at the accountant's office by 30th September.

ACCOUNTING GUIDES

I have always worked closely with my clients and aim to empower them so that they know more about their accounts and can do more themselves. With this in mind, I have devised a series of Simple Accountancy Guides so that business owners can do some of the figure work themselves.

Being released in December 2014 and early in 2015

- *Anna's Simple Accounting Guides —The Quick and Easy Guide to Bank Reconciliations*
  Get to grips with your cash flow and know what goes where and why.

- *Anna's Simple Accounting Guides —Budgets*
  Simple and easy to understand

- *Anna's Simple Accounting Guides - Sole-trader or Limited company?*
  Which to choose, why and the pitfalls of both.

Please keep up to date with the guides and what Alan and Bert are up to by liking my Facebook author page.

www.facebook.com/AnnatheauthorGoodwin